Contents

*For Olivia and Zac—never stop playing games**

*Only if you have done your homework <u>and</u> it is not past your bedtime!

2021

www.redvarkpublishing.co.uk

Version 1.00f

Cover artwork by AJ Noon and KS Lawrence

Game & Food Photos by AJ Noon

Illustrations and sanity checks by KS Lawrence (*without whom this entire endeavour would not have been possible, and who wants to be paid in tea*).

All pictures of games are from my own (AJ Noon) personal collection and are not endorsed or sponsored in any way. No meeples were harmed in the production of this book.

There is a full list of the games, and their manufacturers, played during the compilation of this book at the end, though don't look if you are planning on doing the quiz!

Front Cover Background Game: Catan (3-4 players) by Catan Studio

Introduction

A gaming session is one of the best ways to spend a few hours; for the escapism, the social aspect and, apparently, some people play competitively.

One of the things that helps bring a session to life is having something to snack on whilst playing. I'm not talking about a full three-course dinner (only because I don't have a large enough table to game <u>and</u> dine at the same time), but something that is quick and easy to prepare, whether hot or cold, that will keep your stomach full and your wits sharp. Though you can buy a zillion different pre-made snacks and treats, it is nice to be able to offer your fellow players something with a home-made feel.

The recipes in this book are here to give you a starting point, all can easily be tweaked or customised to suit your own preferred flavours, and are easily transported should you be taking a dish to a friends' if you are not hosting. Apart from the 'Alcohol' section at the end, all of these recipes are simple enough to get the kids involved, so if it is a family event they can help with (or do all!) the preparation.

If you are taking food to the house of a fellow gamer, check with them which foods they find acceptable (and not just for vegetarian and gluten-free options). Games cost a lot of money, and many gamers get twitchy at the thought of grease or sauces around their favourite pastime, so see what their arrangements for food are. If they are serving the food between games, then go ahead with the cheese straws and curry dips, but if they are looking for snacks that can be eaten during play, look to the wraps and/or houmous dips.

Whether you are just providing finger food or looking to theme sustenance around your favourite games, I hope this gives you some ideas and enhances your gaming sessions.

AJN: writerajnoon@gmail.com

A huge thanks goes out to all the crafty creatives, the incredible illustrators, and the demonic designers who lovingly create the games and accessories that we are passionate about.

Symbology

On each recipe card you will find a 'stats' bar. This gives you an at-a-glance guide to the snack's properties and preparation.

Please note that most of the recipes have mod suggestions so you can increase or reduce the spiciness, make it vegetarian, and more.

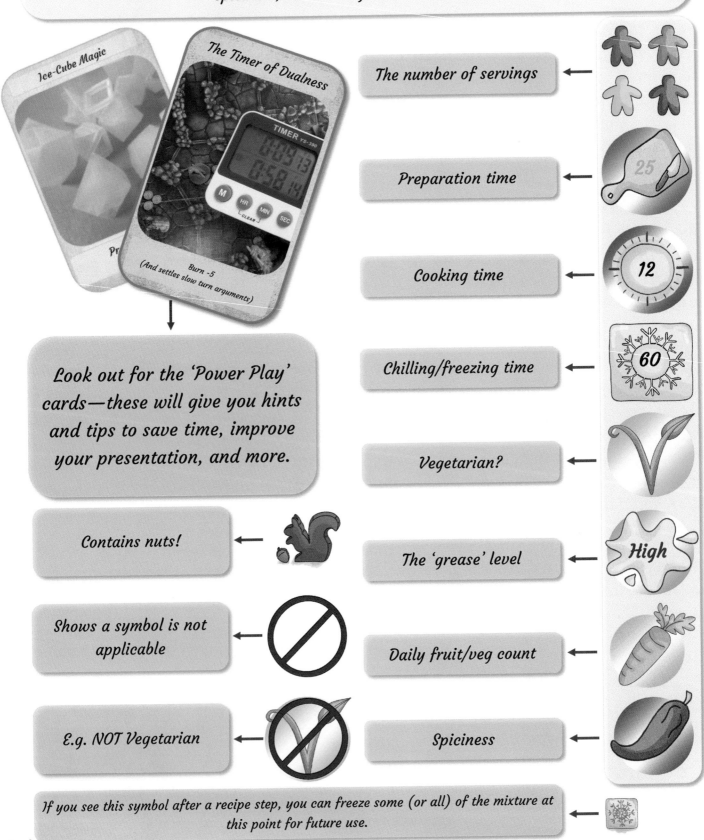

Ice-Cube Magic

The Timer of Dualness

TIMER YS-390

M   HR   MIN   SEC
CLEAR

Burn -5
(And settles slow turn arguments)

Look out for the 'Power Play' cards—these will give you hints and tips to save time, improve your presentation, and more.

The number of servings

Preparation time

Cooking time

Chilling/freezing time

Vegetarian?

Contains nuts!

The 'grease' level

Shows a symbol is not applicable

Daily fruit/veg count

E.g. NOT Vegetarian

Spiciness

25

12

60

High

If you see this symbol after a recipe step, you can freeze some (or all) of the mixture at this point for future use.

Essentials, Time-Savers, and Useful Gear

You want to maximise your gaming-time rather than spend it in the kitchen, so here are a couple of tips and time-saving devices that may help. If you are playing new games, or have players who may not be familiar with your selections, I recommend that you find some YouTube walkthroughs and email them the links a few days beforehand. Even if they watch them in the taxi on the way over at least they will have a feel for how a game plays before seeing it for the first time.

Essentials

The first essential is to check your guests for allergies and intolerances. If you devise a menu in advance, then email it to your guests to give them a chance to send you feedback. Vegetarian, vegan, pescatarian, peanuts, tomatoes, wheat, milk and eggs are the most common things to check for with your guests, but there are others out there that could trip you up so please check with your diners first (even if you think you know them well, it is worth double-checking). Keep an eye out for the squirrel meeple for a nut warning.

The second essential is cocktail sticks. As long as your snack can be skewered, then these are absolutely the best option for keeping fingers away from the food, so grease and sauces don't get transferred to your precious gaming components.

The third is wet-wipes. Should there be a spillage, or greasy fingers cannot be avoided, then these are ideal for wiping down. More importantly, they are great (and non-destructive) for quickly wiping game pieces, cards, and even the boards, if required.

The fourth is kitchen-roll or dry tissues. Have these to hand, especially if you have your drinks on the same table as the game pieces.

If you are playing, eating, and drinking in a small area, consider investing in a dice-tower to prevent errant rolls. These come in many shapes and forms, and you can buy them pre-printed, custom designed, or plain for you to paint up as you want. You can also get double-sided ones, so if it is placed in the middle of a table two sides can use it easily. Should you have a gamer in your midst whose dice-rolling action is questionable, these also help eliminate raised eyebrows and accusations.

The final recommended items, though some may say these are compulsory, are card sleeves to protect your games. For those with large game collections this may not be financially viable, but if you at least protect your favourite games then you are helping to extend their lifetime.

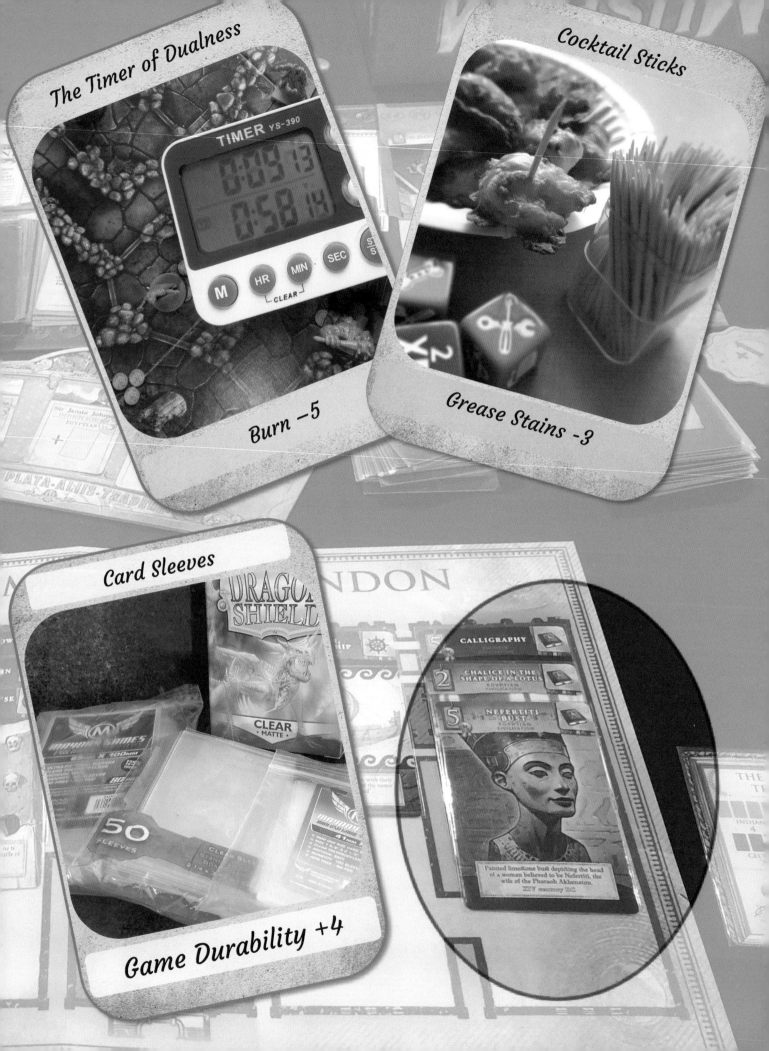

The Timer of Dualness

Burn −5

Cocktail Sticks

Grease Stains -3

Card Sleeves

Game Durability +4

Preparation

Getting everything perfect for your gaming session can be time-consuming, but this is not _Masterchef_ or _Bake Off_ so we are more than happy to use any device or trick to save time. It is worth doing as much as possible in advance so you can spend more time gaming with your friends.

 If you are preparing veg, you can buy it pre-sliced/diced in the frozen section at the supermarket, and we've found the little pots of pre-diced frozen herbs (chilli, garlic, ginger etc) invaluable.

If you prefer to prepare your own, and don't have ninja knife skills, there are a range of cheap mechanical slicers and dicers that are perfect for the job.

 Pastry: buy it ready-rolled from the store.

As well as individual spices, you can now get a wide variety of blended rubs and mixes from your local supermarket, which are ideal time and space savers. Look for peri peri, Italian herb, Cajun, and chipotle.

 You can buy packs of popcorn for the microwave, but your own popcorn maker is a handy thing to have (and more child-friendly than a pan). Once you have made your popcorn, you can add a huge variety of toppings to it, either savoury, sweet, or half-and-half.

Serving

Consider whether you are going to break your gaming session up by having food during an interval or, if you don't dare pause in the middle of a Zombicide marathon, you will want to have food out for guests to eat as you play. If guests will be eating throughout play, make sure your cocktail sticks, baby-wipes, and tissues are to hand.

If you are serving hot food, then food warmers are affordable and easily available. You can buy electric versions (at a premium), but the basic ones use tea-lights to keep each section warm and are cheap and effective. The candle flame is enclosed within the unit so are perfectly safe, and they come in a range of sizes, from smaller warmers for a single plate to those that can handle four at a time.

To go with a food warmer, a set of Balti dishes work perfectly. They are inexpensive, easy to clean, and just the right size for smaller portions of curries, dips (hot or cold), stews and more.

If you are serving hot food in individual dishes (such as the nachos), don't forget your placemats to protect your table and the hands of your guests. There is a broad range of branded mats available, just make sure they have some level of thermal protection.

Card Racks

Tidiness +2

(although also Cheat +1)

Dice Tower

Spillage Save +5

Spare Dice

Over-stretching -2

(Spillage Save +2)

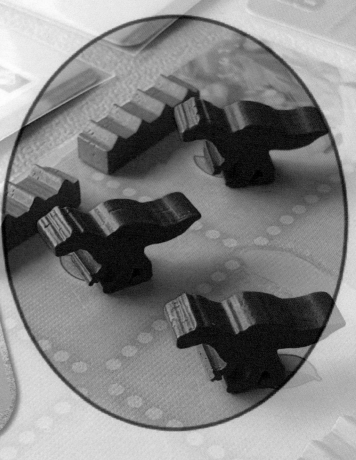

Theming and Extras

If you are theming your evening, don't forget the napkins, straws, and even wine-glass charms so everyone knows whose glass is whose. If the evening is more relaxed (and you want less washing up), thermal insulators for cans will help keep them cool, as well as showing to whom it belongs.

 If you want to add a theme to your session, then there are a wide variety of silicone moulds available, though usually delivered from China so order in plenty of time. These can be used for making chocolates, vodka jellies, ice-cubes, and more.

There is a range of excellent can holders (which have an adapter to take soda cans or beer cans) that are 3D printable and come themed for different RPG roles, such as Wizard, Dwarf, Dragon and more. You can get these either as the 3D files to print yourself or pre-printed and they are made by Ars Moriendi 3D (www.arsmoriendi3d.com).

 There is a thriving market on Etsy.com for quirky game-related products: Do you need Carcassonne or Magic the Gathering coasters? Catan whisky glasses? Meeple candles? Edible Zombie cake-toppers? All these, and more, can be found with a little searching.

Apps like Ambient Mixer let you programme your own atmosphere to replicate a medieval city, market, castle, or sea voyage. I can find it distracting if it is too loud, but people have curated playlists for specific games. Head over to Spotify for lists that cover Gloomhaven, Warhammer, D&D, Viking themed games, and more. You can also make your own playlists using YouTube or your iPod, but watch out for the adverts now on YouTube which can interrupt your gaming. There are also several soundboard apps and streaming radio stations aimed at gamers.

 For transporting games, there are bags designed specifically for holding (and protecting) games, making transportation easier. Some are simple padded shoulder bags that will hold a couple of regular sized games, some are complex, multi-compartment beasts that can protect your copy of Pandemic through a nuclear attack.

There are also box bands available in a range of sizes. These are kinder on your boxes than elastic bands, and can be picked up pretty cheaply. These are very helpful if you have boxes filled with slippery sleeved cards that are just waiting for the opportunity to escape.

Box Bands

Lost Pieces Save +5

Mythic Mugs

Themed 3D Can Holders

Spillage Save +3

Card Dealer

Tidiness +2

Checklists

The Basics

- ☐ Invitations Sent?
- ☐ Allergies Checked?
- ☐ Enough Chairs/Seats?
- ☐ Enough Glasses?
- ☐ Serving Plates & Bowls
- ☐ Cocktail Sticks
- ☐ Wet Wipes & Tissues
- ☐ Dips & Dippers

The Extras

- ☐ Email YouTube walkthroughs for new games
- ☐ Background Music
- ☐ Themed Napkins/Décor
- ☐ Ice for Drinks
- ☐ Table Protector
- ☐ Break/Eating Time Determined?
- ☐ Blankets—people like different temperatures so have a blanket or two to hand
- ☐ Extra Cushions—some people need more padding!
- ☐ Swear Box—If you have younger people playing you may want a swear box to help keep the adults in line

The Games

- ☐ Pen & Paper (if scoring)
- ☐ Spare Dice
- ☐ Quick Games (Time Fillers)
- ☐ Main Game(s)
- ☐ Backup Game (in case you finish early or want to change)

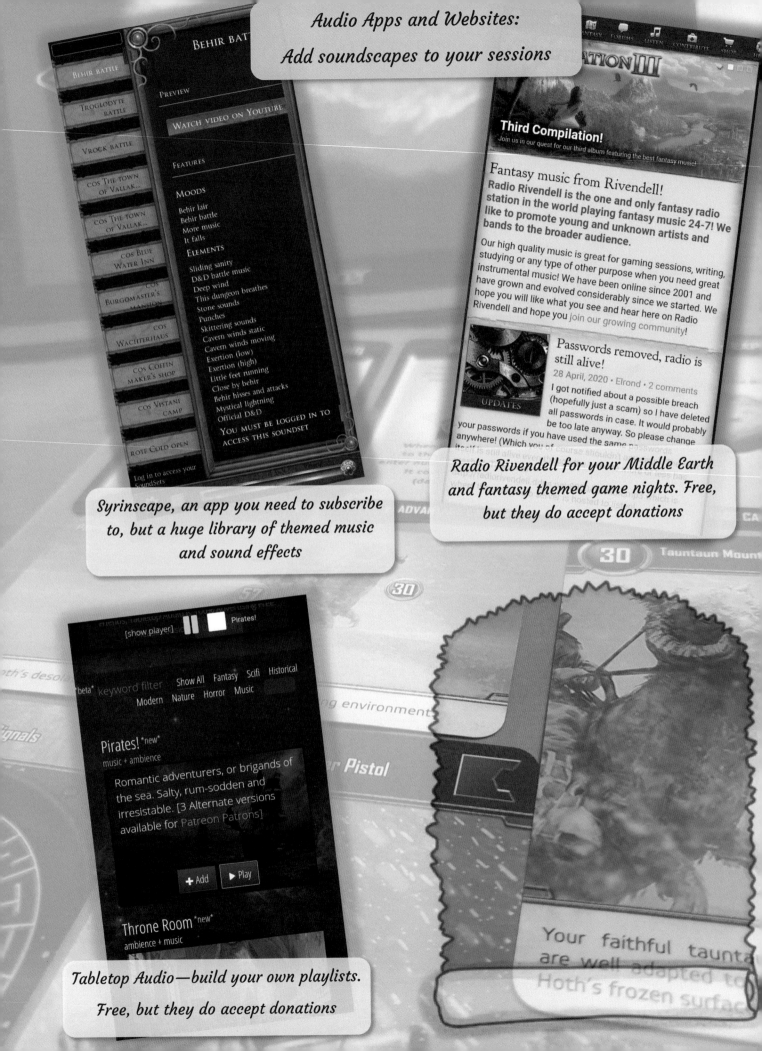

Audio Apps and Websites:
Add soundscapes to your sessions

BEHIR BATTLE

BEHIR BATTLE
TROGLODYTE BATTLE
VROCK BATTLE
COS THE TOWN OF VALLAK...
COS THE TOWN OF VALLAK...
COS BLUE WATER INN
COS BURGOMASTER'S MANSION
COS WACHTERHAUS
COS COFFIN MAKER'S SHOP
COS VISTANI CAMP
ROTE COLD OPEN

Log in to access your SoundSets

PREVIEW

WATCH VIDEO ON YOUTUBE

FEATURES

MOODS
Behir lair
Behir battle
More music
It falls

ELEMENTS
Sliding sanity
D&D battle music
Deep wind
This dungeon breathes
Stone sounds
Punches
Skittering sounds
Cavern winds static
Cavern winds moving
Exertion (low)
Exertion (high)
Little feet running
Close by behir
Behir hisses and attacks
Mystical lightning
Official D&D
YOU MUST BE LOGGED IN TO ACCESS THIS SOUNDSET

Syrinscape, an app you need to subscribe to, but a huge library of themed music and sound effects

ATION III

Third Compilation!
Join us in our quest for our third album featuring the best fantasy music!

Fantasy music from Rivendell!
Radio Rivendell is the one and only fantasy radio station in the world playing fantasy music 24-7! We like to promote young and unknown artists and bands to the broader audience.

Our high quality music is great for gaming sessions, writing, studying or any type of other purpose when you need great instrumental music! We have been online since 2001 and have grown and evolved considerably since we started. We hope you will like what you see and hear here on Radio Rivendell and hope you join our growing community!

Passwords removed, radio is still alive!
28 April, 2020 • Elrond • 2 comments
I got notified about a possible breach (hopefully just a scam) so I have deleted all passwords in case. It would probably be too late anyway. So please change your passwords if you have used the same passwords anywhere! (Which you of course shouldn't...

UPDATES

Radio Rivendell for your Middle Earth and fantasy themed game nights. Free, but they do accept donations

[show player]   ▮▮ ☐   Pirates!

beta keyword filter   Show All Fantasy Scifi Historical
Modern Nature Horror Music

Pirates! *new*
music + ambience

Romantic adventurers, or brigands of the sea. Salty, rum-sodden and irresistable. [3 Alternate versions available for Patreon Patrons]

+ Add   ▶ Play

Throne Room *new*
ambience + music

Tabletop Audio—build your own playlists.
Free, but they do accept donations

30 Tauntaun Moun

Your faithful taunta
are well adapted to
Hoth's frozen surfac

Conversion Help

So many countries, so many measuring systems...

Solids

Metric	Imperial
10g	.25 oz
25g	1 oz
50g	1.75 oz
75g	2.75 oz
100g	2.5 oz
200g	7 oz
250g	9 oz
300g	10.5 oz

Temperatures

Celsius	Fahrenheit	Gas
65 °C	150 °F	
93 °C	200 °F	1/4
150 °C	300 °F	2
160 °C	325 °F	3
180 °C	350 °F	4
190 °C	375 °F	5
200 °C	395 °F	6
220 °C	425 °F	7

Liquids

Cups	Imperial	Metric
1/16 cup	.5 fl oz	15 ml
1/8 cup	1 fl oz	30 ml
1/4 cup	2 fl oz	60 ml
1/3 cup	3 fl oz	80 ml
1/2 cup	4 fl oz	120 ml
2/3 cup	5 fl oz	160 ml
3/4 cup	6 fl oz	180 ml
1 cup	8 fl oz	240 ml

Present Idea

DAYS OF WONDER PRESENTS
TICKET TO RIDE

Game Posters

Carry Bags

Travel Protection +2

Let's Get Theming...

Cheap Themed Napkins
Presentation +2

Roll Your Own Menu

Not sure what to prepare for your guests? Then grab your D6 and make a lucky throw:

Vegetarian

1—Nachos

2—Cheese Carca-Scones

3—Buffalo Cauliflower Wings

4—Cheese Tikkis

5—Spinach Crescent Roll

6—Chilli Garlic Bread

Carnivore

1—Kathi Kebab Rolls

2—Croissant Hot Dogs

3—Mexican Chicken Kebabs

4—Spice Mini-Meatballs

5—Mini Toad-in-the-Holes

6—Sausage Rolls

Sweet-tooth

1—Millionaire's Shortbread

2—Honey Biscuits

3—Muffins

4—Resource Cube Fudge

5—Chocolate Swirl Tart

6—Flapjacks

D6 Heat Modifier

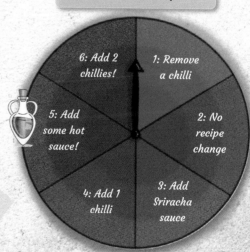

6: Add 2 chillies!

1: Remove a chilli

5: Add some hot sauce!

2: No recipe change

4: Add 1 chilli

3: Add Sriracha sauce

Other Resources

Reviews

https://boardgamegeek.com/ is one of the most established and recognised review sites for board games. As well as having game specs and user reviews, they also have aggregated ratings, details of expansions and edition variations, and photos. If you are considering a new game this should be one of your first ports of call.

Boardgamequest.com and Gamesradar.com also provide similar reviews and ratings.

YouTube Tutorials and Walk-Throughs

Geek & Sundry, The Dice Tower, Watch It Played, and The Rules Girl are some of the most popular channels on YouTube, and if you are considering a game I recommend watching it being played first (if you can't play it beforehand at your local club/cafe).

Magazines

Tabletop Gaming Magazine is our favourite hard-copy gaming magazine. The monthly subscription makes a great present for the gamer in your life. They also do a yearly magazine reviewing all the new game releases for that year.

https://www.tabletopgaming.co.uk/

Card Sleeve Finders

There are plenty of online resources to help you find the right size sleeves required for your games. Sites, such as boardgamegeek and sleeveyourgames, list sleeving requirements by game, and there are apps for your phone as well:

https://www.maydaygames.com/pages/sleeves-by-game

https://www.sleeveyourgames.com/

https://boardgamegeek.com/geeklist/164572/card-sleeve-sizes-games

The Boardgame Quiz

Can you identify the boardgames in the backgrounds on the following pages? Fill in your answers below, then check your score on page 106.

Page 6 _____

Page 8 _____

Page 10 _____

Page 12 _____

Page 14 _____

Page 18 _____

Page 22 _____

Page 24 _____

Page 26 _____

Page 28 _____

Page 30 _____

Page 32 _____

Page 34 _____

Page 36 _____

Page 38 _____

Page 40 _____

Page 42 _____

Page 44 _____

Page 46 _____

Page 48 _____

Page 50 _____

Page 52 _____

Page 54 _____

Page 56 _____

Page 58 _____

Page 60 _____

Page 62 _____

Page 66 _____

Page 68 _____

Page 70 _____

Page 72 _____

Page 74 _____

Page 76 _____

Page 78 _____

Page 80 _____

Page 82 _____

Page 84 _____

Page 88 _____

Page 90 _____

Page 92 _____

Page 94 _____

Page 96 _____

Page 98 _____

Page 110 _____

Your Score

/44

LEMON AND SLIME

Alice Ironheart

Cheat Card

Frozen Herbs—easy to use, no waste, and no time lost in preparation

Presentation

Meeple Cheeseboard!
Yes Please :)

Watch out!

You think you've rolled a 6, then the Dice Devil tilts it!

Dips #1

You can make your own dips from scratch, but that is valuable time lost so I suggest you buy them ready-made. The range and quality of available dips from the supermarkets and—increasingly—local butchers and artisan shops, is pretty comprehensive, and there always seems to be a new dip that is all the rage for a month or two.

As already stated, the aim of this book is to give you more gaming time and less kitchen time, so here's a quick summary of some of the more popular dips to look out for in case you are not familiar with them:

Sweet Chilli Dipping Sauce

One of the best all-rounders, this sauce is brilliant with chicken, fish and beef. You can get it in a range of strengths, or you can just save the free ones from fast-food restaurants.

Houmous

A nice creamy dip, available in a range of sub-flavours. The red pepper version tends to be sweeter, whilst the Moroccan has an earthier, spicier taste to it. Beetroot houmous is great with vegetarian wraps and breadsticks.

Dips—Cheat and buy them

Tzatziki

This dip is perfect for cooling curries and any of the cauliflower dishes (such as the Buffalo Cauliflower Wings). It also works well with the pitta dippers.

Cheddar Cheese and Chive

Tangy, thick, and great with potato skins, and Yorkshire Puddings (honestly).

Dips #2

Guacamole

Smooth or chunky, it goes well with anything Mexican. Add it to a salad for extra body, as a garnish on veggie burgers, or pair with smoked salmon on thin slices of crusty French bread.

Salsa (Cool or Hot)

Salsas go well with wraps, chicken dishes, baked potatoes, or add it to slow-cooked beef dishes.

Baba Ghanoush

Made with aubergine (eggplant if you're in the USA), it is great for dipping vegetable sticks into, spreading onto pitta or flatbreads, or even adding to toasted ham sandwiches.

Thousand Island Dressing

A little sweeter than some of the other sauces, add it to burgers and salads. This works better as a topping rather than as a dip.

Satay Sauce

My own personal favourite, this peanut-based sauce is great for spreading onto chicken (before or after cooking).

 *Remember to check with guests for allergies with this one!

We All Need A Dip

Scoop it into a bowl —or leave it in the plastic if you don't want to wash up!

Dippers

For shorter gaming sessions, providing a range of cooked dishes may be too much, so you may just want to set out a few dips (as listed above) and some dippers.

Breadsticks

Crunchy and great for dipping, you can get plain breadsticks that let your dips do the talking. Go for mini, gluten-free, wheat-bran, or sesame-seed coated varieties.

Vegetable and Fruit Sticks & Squares

Carrots, cucumbers, peppers, and celery can be sliced into sticks and served with dips. Fruit tends to be sticker/juicier but works well if you cube it and spike it onto wooden skewers (like a kebab). Melons, pineapples, strawberries, orange segments, kiwi fruit, bananas, and even blueberries work well. Try dipping them in natural Greek yoghurt (if it doesn't make it feel too much like breakfast!).

Tortilla Chips, Pitta Triangles, and Mini-Naans

All are crunchy, with plenty of different flavour options, so mix-and-match a few different bags to create your own combinations, or get smaller bowls so guests can keep themselves topped up.

Sweet pastry cases—great for making mini-mousses, millionaires shortbread, lemon meringues, and more (and leaves nothing to wash up).

Need Bowls?

If you are lacking in suitable bowls for dips, get yourself to the charity shops!

Need a Table?

Go to Geeknson.co.uk to see an impressive range of bespoke tables tailored to your gaming needs.

Make trays from puff pastry (prick the bottom so it does not rise too much)

Edible Containers

Food needn't be served on a plate or in a bowl, you can make the container edible as well:

Potato skins are the most delicious options. Scrub the potatoes clean (do not peel), and bake for an hour at 200°C (180 fan). Cut the potatoes lengthways in half, hollow them out (saving the insides for another dish, such as the Crispy Mash Balls on Page 57) then brush the skins lightly with olive oil. Cook them for a further 10 minutes at 220°C (200 fan) so they crisp up.

Serve them with a filling of your choice. The chilli and curry recipes work well served like this.

Crispy skins waiting to be filled...

As they take some time to cook, you can freeze them, either empty or with a filling, ready for reheating at a future session. I usually cook eight to ten spuds at a time, then freeze them with two different fillings (one vegetarian and one meat).

Yorkshire puddings also make a great serving option. Buy them frozen, heat them up and put in a spoonful or two of a thick curry or a stew and you have a great snack and less washing up.

Tortillas, Indian rotis and chapatis, and pitta breads all make great containers for kebabs, thick curries, or even just a spicy salad.

If you want to be really healthy, try using a large lettuce leaf. Banana leaves make a good container but are NOT edible.

For sweet items, meringue nests, small pastry cases, edible cupcake cases, and chocolate cups can all be used to hold your creations.

Tortilla and taco edible containers

Fruit skewers, healthier than crisps

Keep It Warm

A dish warmer with Balti dishes. Candle or electric versions are available

Card Holder

Lurkers

Frox Raider
Mark 1

1   4

Tidiness +1

Stay up-to-date...

RATED: EVERY SPIEL DE JAH
WHAT CAN WE LEARN FROM THE BIGGEST

table
GAMING
BOARD GAMES | CARD GAMES | MI

CHIVALRY
& SORCERY
The most complete
medieval world on
your tabletop

DUNGEONS &

MY
OR

News +3

Savoury

Dough Saver

Freeze unused dough for up to 1 month

Overlap the triangles...

Fill and fold...

Ready to tear-and-share

Make It Personal...

Companies such as Sculpteo (above) will do 3D scans and printed figurines of yourself—perfect for making you the hero of Zombicide...

Orc

Spinach Dip Crescent Roll

Ingredients:

50g of fresh spinach

350g croissant dough

30g cream cheese

10g sour cream

A pinch of garlic powder

A pinch of onion powder

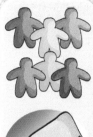

Method:

Pre-heat the oven to 200 degrees (180 fan).

Put the cream cheese, sour cream, and garlic and onion powders into a bowl and mix well.

Add the spinach and lightly mix to combine.

Lay out the triangular croissant dough into a ring shape with the points of the triangles facing out and the corners overlapping to join it up.

Place the mixture around the circle, then wrap the triangles over to touch the inner edge (see picture).

Bake in the oven for 16 minutes.

Mods:

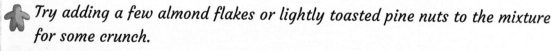

Try adding a few almond flakes or lightly toasted pine nuts to the mixture for some crunch.

Smoked salmon works well if you want to get your essential fatty oil.

For a salty hit, add cooked and chopped bacon. Or for a fresher taste a little mint and coriander.

Cutting Cauli

Cut a cone out from the base of the cauliflower and the florets will come apart easily and cleanly

Messy...

Ally, Hero

1-4: Move this card up to 1 space. Place up to 1 card in the loot row or loot deck. Attack X equals the loot's monster, this ~

Keep your gr~

©2019 Hypercub~

But nice

Watch out for Stains!

Spices such as turmeric will stain fingers and cards

What the...?

Mulligan: When the other players allow you to re-take a poorly taken move

Eurogames: Heavy on strategy, low on luck (i.e. no dice rolling)

Push-Your-Luck: Take a safe score? Or try for more at the risk of losing all?

Roll-and-Write: Write onto the board/player cards as you progress (usually with an erasable marker)

Legacy: The next scenario for a game is affected directly by the one you previously played

Buffalo Cauliflower Wings

Ingredients:

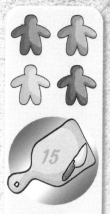

1 cauliflower, cut into bite-sized chunks

200g of cornflour

100ml water

100ml milk

2 teaspoons of garlic powder

1 teaspoon of cumin

1 teaspoon of paprika

Salt and pepper

25g of butter

200 ml hot sauce (Frank's Buffalo Wings, Encona hot, Heinz Firecracker)

Method:

Pre-heat the oven to 200 degrees (180 fan) and line a baking tray with baking paper.

Mix the flour, water, milk, and spice together to form a thick batter.

Dip each cauliflower floret in the batter, covering well. Gently shake off the excess batter then place on the baking tray.

Cook for 20 minutes, turning over half-way through, then place in a large bowl.

Gently melt the butter and the hot sauce together, stir well, then brush the cauliflower pieces with the sauce mix.

Place back on the baking tray and cook for a further 15 minutes.

Mods:

 Sprinkle on some mozzarella for the last five minutes of cooking for a creamier finish.

To add more heat use curry powder or a Mexican spice mix instead of the paprika and cumin.

Marinade Warning!

You can use leftover marinade for basting as you cook, but you cannot save it for later use (cross-contamination)

Avoid 'Freezer Burn'

Rather than freeze items in the packs they came in, wrap them up tightly to eliminate air and avoid the burn

The Hand of Fate!
(aka Andrew V.) →

Perfect for a tortilla pocket!

Purchases

Prison

Kathi Kebab Rolls

Ingredients:

250g chicken breasts (cut into strips)

150ml Greek yoghurt

4 parathas (or tortillas)

1 onion and 1 pepper, finely sliced

Juice of 1 lemon

1 finely chopped thumb of ginger

2 tablespoons Tandoori masala

Half a tablespoon of turmeric

2 finely chopped cloves of garlic

Salt and pepper to taste

Method:

Place the chicken, yoghurt, tandoori masala, lemon juice and turmeric into a bowl, cover, and place in the fridge to marinate—ideally for two hours (or longer).

When you are ready to cook, heat a pan (medium heat) with a little oil and lightly fry the ginger and garlic.

Add the onion and pepper, cook for two minutes, then add the chicken (make sure you add all of the sauce from the marinade as well).

Stir well, and cook for 8 minutes.

Heat the parathas in a microwave (10 seconds), then fill each one with the cooked mixture and serve.

Mods:

 These are great as you can make them vegetarian simply by swapping the chicken for paneer and cauliflower chunks.

As you cook, if the mixture starts to look too dry, add more of the Greek yoghurt.

Instead of parathas, you can also use tortillas or wraps, whatever you have to hand (or prefer).

Pre-Mixed Spices

Dragon rub
Spicy Taco mix
Thai rub
Chimichurri

2

Flavour +4

Prep Time −2

Serve in pirate loot boxes?

Sleeving Gloomhaven

Will to Live −2

Soak your skewers!

Mexican Chicken Kebabs

Ingredients:

Wooden skewers (min 6)

4 chicken breasts

1 lime (juiced, and finely grated rind)

3 tablespoons of chipotle paste

2 crushed garlic cloves

1 tablespoon of honey

1 tablespoon of olive oil

Method:

Add all of the ingredients (except the chicken and the skewers) into a bowl and mix well.

Place the chicken breasts between two sheets of clingfilm and then bash them with a rolling pin repeatedly until you have a uniform flatness of around 1.5 centimetres.

Remove from the clingfilm, then cut the chicken into strips. Place the strips in the marinade, stir well, then cover and set aside in the fridge for at least one hour.

Place the kebab skewers into water and leave to soak (otherwise they will burn during cooking) for 20 minutes.

Thread the marinated chicken strips onto the skewers, then grill for 6-8 minutes until cooked.

Mods:

You can add chorizo slices to the skewers, or slices of vegetables such as mushrooms and peppers.

Leaving the chicken in the marinade for longer (overnight is ideal) will really allow the flavours to penetrate the chicken. Increase the spiciness by adding chilli flakes to the marinade.

Oil Me Up

Make your own flavoured oil—Try adding dried chillies to a small bottle of olive oil and leave for a week to flavour

Money Saver

DUNGEON EXTRAVAGANZA

HUMBLE RPG BOOK BUNDLE: 5TH EDITION DUNGEON EXTRAVAGANZA

We're bringing serious 5e tabletop adventures to you in our latest bundle! Get ebooks like *Amazing Adventures 5E Quickstarter, For the Love of Valentine,* and *The Dragon Isles 5 Map Set.* Plus, your purchase helps support the Navy-Marine Corps Relief Society!

AWESOME STUFF • PAY £0.72 OR MORE • DRM-FREE • MULTI-FORMAT • 10,4

GET THE BUNDLE

TIME LEFT

02	07	46	52
days	hours	min	sec

Keep an eye on HumbleBundle.com, who do offers on D&D resources (digital and print) and Steam bundles, also raising money for charity

Feed Me...

Broccoli Tikkis

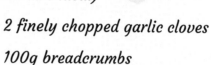

Ingredients:

300g broccoli (very small pieces)

250g potatoes, washed and peeled

100g grated cheese (Cheddar or Red Leicester are ideal)

2 finely chopped onions

2 finely chopped garlic cloves

2 finely chopped chillies

100g breadcrumbs

Salt and pepper

Method:

Boil and mash the potatoes, then put them to one side.

Lightly brown the onions and garlic, then add the broccoli and chillies and fry for four minutes.

Add the cheese, salt and pepper to taste, and stir well, before allowing to cool.

Once cooled, add the mashed potatoes and mix to combine, then form 8 round patties. ❄️

Coat in the breadcrumbs, then fry in a large frying pan until both sides are golden brown.

Serve with a dip such as tzatziki or houmous.

Mods:

 Swap 50g of cheddar cheese for mozzarella to add some real ooze to the tikkis.

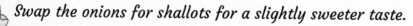

 Swap the onions for shallots for a slightly sweeter taste.

Add spices to the mix before frying, such as chaat masala, tikka, or tandoori.

 For the carnivores, add finely chopped bacon or chorizo at the first frying stage. These can be frozen, once bread-crumbed, for up to one month.

Chill your batter before using. This also applies to pancake batter

Ready to go into the oven...

The finished treat—why not giant size them?

Cheat Card

Drop a cooked chipolata onto a frozen Yorkshire pud batte mix.

When it is cooked you will then have space to add sauce or gravy

Mini Toad-in-the-Holes

Ingredients:

12 cocktail sausages

100g plain flour

2 medium eggs

Salt and pepper

175ml milk

1 tbsp English mustard

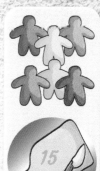

Method:

Pre-heat the oven to 200 degrees (180 fan) and put the sausages on a tray in the oven for 12 minutes, turning once. At the same time, take your muffin tin (or mini loaf tins), add a teaspoon of oil, and put it on a different shelf in the oven.

Mix the flour, milk, eggs, and mustard (ideally with an electric whisk) until you have a smooth batter. If the batter seems too thick (gloopy) add small amounts of cold water to help thin it. Chill the batter for 10 minutes.

Carefully take the sausages and the hot muffin tin out of the oven and add equal amounts of batter to each hole, then add 2 sausages to the centre of each.

Place back in the oven for 15 minutes or until golden brown.

Mods:

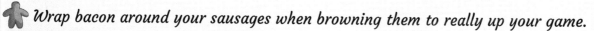

Wrap bacon around your sausages when browning them to really up your game.

Make a thick onion gravy to cover them with (not great around games though), or supply a horse-radish sauce for dipping.

You can use herby or spicy sausages cut to size instead of cocktail sausages.

What the...?

Ameritrash: Highly themed, miniature and dice heavy

Co-op: Not the shop—games where the players have to work together rather than against each other

Drafting: There is a shared resource of cards all players can pick from, rather than individual decks

Social Deduction: Who did it? Which player is the werewolf/spy/traitor?

Solitaire/Solo: Games that can be played by one player (very useful to have in a pandemic!)

Don't forget the quick-play games to add a bit of energy to your session. Get Bit and Zombie Dice are 2 suggestions

BRONZ

Sprinkle with some finely sliced chillies?

Or serve in a tortilla bowl?

Dyslexic?

Check out Geeknative.com for dyslexic friendly D&D character sheets

TIDAL PALACE

Vegan Bean Chilli

Ingredients:

400g chopped tomatoes

400g red kidney beans in chilli sauce

500g sweet potatoes

1 pepper

400g mixed beans

6 spring onions

2 crushed garlic cloves

Chilli flakes to taste (half a teaspoon is a good starting point)

1 tablespoon each of mixed herbs, coriander, cumin, and brown sugar

Salt and pepper to taste

Method:

Put everything except the lime juice into a slow cooker, stir it well, then cook on high for 4 hours.

Stir once an hour (not required, but helpful).

Serve with rice, tortillas, nachos, or even crackers to use as scoops.

Sprinkle a little fresh lime juice over the top when serving.

The chilli can be frozen after cooking and stored for up to two months.

Mods:

If you like it hotter, rather than just adding chillies, try adding some chipotle powder—this has a bit of a kick and also adds depth to the flavour.

If you have made it hotter, a dd a sprinkle of cheese or sour cream, when serving.

If you want to up the veg count, add a couple of finely sliced onions or carrots.

To add more depth to the flavour, add two teaspoons of smoked paprika. To turn it into a meat-dish, add 500g lean minced beef (brown it off first in a frying pan) and a beef stock cube.

Curry Aid

If you don't have spices to hand, use a jar of pre-prepared curry paste.

Curries benefit from long cooking times to allow the flavour to develop.

Make Your Own?

Companies such as www.thegamecrafter.com can produce custom designed and printed meeples, tokens, and more.

Serve in a Yorkshire pudding?

Present Ideas

Journals to record your worlds and adventures can add heft to your records, and memories.

Chickpea Curry

Ingredients:

400g chickpeas (drained)

400g chopped tomatoes

500g cauliflower (diced)

100g peas (frozen or fresh)

1 onion, diced

1 cup of water

1 tablespoon each of curry powder, cumin, turmeric

200g Brussel sprouts

1 pepper, diced

1 veggie stock cube

Salt and pepper

Method:

Place everything into the slow cooker except the peas.

Stir well, then cook on high for four hours.

After 2 hours, stir and add water as required (it should be no more than 1 cup maximum, you are aiming for a thick consistency, not runny).

15 minutes before serving, add the peas.

Serve with rice, chips, or lightly grilled slices of naan bread to use as scoops.

This can be frozen once cooked for up to two months, or stored in an airtight container for two days in the fridge.

Mods:

 As with any curry, you can swap the cauliflower for your preferred veg (if using broccoli only add it with 1 hour of cooking to go).

 The addition of lamb or chicken (brown it first in a frying pan) turns this tasty veggie treat into a meat feast.

Tofu Types

Look for a firm tofu, not the silken variety. Silken tofu is used for dips and smoothies, whereas firm is used more as the meat substitute (*silken left, firm right*)

Tantalise Your Tofu

Use different oils when cooking with Tofu to get maximum flavour. Sesame oil for a more savoury taste, coconut oil for a sweeter taste.

If you've not cooked with Tofu before you need to get plenty of flavour into the coating

Press that Tofu to drain it before use

Panko breadcrumbs makes them crispy

Tofu Nuggets

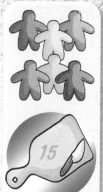

Ingredients:

350g firm Tofu (drained and pressed)

50g of plain flour

50g Panko breadcrumbs

150ml of non-dairy milk

1 teaspoon each of paprika, mustard powder, garlic powder and onion powder

Salt and black pepper to taste

Method:

Pre-heat the oven to 200 degrees (180 fan).

To make the batter, mix together the milk, the flour, and a pinch of salt and allow to rest for 5-10 minutes.

In a bowl, combine the breadcrumbs, paprika, mustard powder, garlic powder, onion powder, salt, and pepper.

Cut the Tofu into the size of nugget you require, then dip one into the batter. Roll the nugget in the breadcrumb mix until it is evenly coated, and then place on a lined baking tray. Repeat until all the nuggets are coated.

Cook in the oven for 20-25 minutes, turning once halfway through.

Mods:

 You can add chilli or curry flavourings to the breadcrumb mix to add a bit of zing.

Try marinating the tofu for an hour with a tikka masala sauce, before coating and cooking.

If you want your nuggets crispier, spray them with a little oil before cooking.

Shaving Ginger

To peel ginger, scrape with the back of a teaspoon—very easy

Aid to Dice

You can find both high visibility dice and braille dice (which also tend to be larger than standard) to aid players with visual impairments.

Cliched...but yummy!

Slow cookers... Perfect for game nights

Spicy Chicken Curry

Ingredients:

3 diced chicken breasts

400g tinned tomatoes

400ml coconut milk

1 piece of chopped ginger

1 chicken stock cube

2 finely chopped onions

3 diced cloves of garlic

3 teaspoons of chilli powder (mild or hot depending on your taste)

1 teaspoon each of cumin, coriander, curry powder, paprika and cinnamon

2 teaspoons of brown sugar

50ml water

Salt and pepper to taste

Method:

In a hot pan brown the chicken and the onions, then add the spices and stir until the chicken is evenly coated.

Put the mix into the slow cooker, then add the stock cube, water, tomatoes, sugar and coconut milk.

Stir well, then cook on high for four hours, stirring once an hour.

Serve with rice, tortillas, nachos, or even crackers as scoops.

Mods:

 For heat, add chillies. For a gluten-free version use a GF stock cube.

 This can be cooked in the oven in a covered pan for a minimum of three hours, though it must be stirred every hour.

 To go vegetarian, swap the chicken for sliced courgette and mushrooms.

Spice Challenge!

Make successively spicier batches of sausage rolls or cheese straws to challenge your friends

Glazy Sunny Afternoons

No glaze vs an egg-yolk glaze on your pastry

Squares...

Or straws?

Chorizo Cheesy Squares

Ingredients:

375g puff pastry sheet

125g grated strong cheddar cheese

2 large (beaten) egg yolks *you can use the whites for meringues on P75

125g grated Mozzarella cheese

125g sliced chorizo

Method:

Pre-heat the oven to 200 degrees (180 fan) and line a tray with baking paper.

Lay the pastry out (landscape) and give it a very quick light roll to stretch it out. Spread the cheese and chorizo across the lower half, then fold the top half of the pastry over it. Sprinkle with black pepper (and finely grated parmesan if you wish), then roll once more to flatten it down and stick the halves together. ❄

Brush the top with the egg wash, then use a sharp knife or a pizza-slicer to cut it vertically into thin strips, then cut horizontally six times to make them into squares (or only cut them horizontally in half to make straws rather than squares).

Place the 'squares' onto the baking tray, keeping a little bit of space between each one to allow them to rise and brown evenly.

Bake in the oven for 12 minutes until golden brown

Mods:

Drop the meat for vegetarians. Prior to folding in half, you can add hot sauces (Sriracha is a favourite), diced chillies, or even just a sprinkling of mustard powder.

To challenge your guests, make several batches, with each batch getting spicier.

A thin layer of a sauce on the cheese, such as mustard, tomato, or Firecracker, adds some heat.

Space your pastry out!

Portioning +2

Sausage Whirls

Try making them like a Swiss roll to make sausage whirls—very quick

Pile Them Up

SCRAP PILE

WARHE
FAKE NEWS

Make two strips—one at the top and one at the bottom

Sausage Rolls

Ingredients:

375g puff pastry

500g sausage meat (or use uncooked sausages by removing the skins)

4 chopped spring onions

2 beaten egg yolks

½ teaspoon of smoked paprika

Salt and pepper

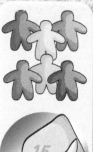

Method:

Pre-heat the oven to 200 degrees (180 fan). Line a tray with baking paper. In a bowl, combine the sausage meat with the spring onions and seasoning, making sure the spicing is evenly spread throughout the mixture.

Lay out your pastry sheet (landscape). One inch from the top edge of the pastry add half the sausage mix from left to right in a tube. Take the top edge of the pastry and roll it over the filling, then roll the whole tube until it has wrapped itself around, which should be half of the pastry. Cut the first tube free, repeat for the remaining half of the pastry. ❄

Tip: Keep the pastry as chilled as possible, if it gets too warm it will be difficult to handle

Brush the tops of the two tubes with the egg wash, then cut into small sausage rolls. Place on the baking tray and bake for 30 minutes.

Mods:

You can buy vegetarian sausage meat instead, or you can make your own vegetarian filling by combing 200g cheddar cheese, 50g of panko breadcrumbs, 4 chopped spring onions, a dollop of double cream, and a dash of paprika. Sauces such as mustard, tomato, or Firecracker, add heat. They work brilliantly with tandoori spices, or try adding sautéed onions, cooked bacon, chillies and/or garlic, chicken tikka or fajita flavourings.

Too coarse...these will burn. Onions must be finely chopped

Wooden Skewers?

Soak them in water for 20 minutes first so they don't burn

Let's eat!

Slicing Nicely

To get neat meat slices, freeze the meat for 30 minutes then cut with a skerrated knife (even a breadknife will work)

Spicy Mini-Meatballs

Ingredients:

800g finely minced beef

1 finely chopped large onion

1 tablespoon of plain flour or cornflour

3 tablespoons of breadcrumbs (you can make your own from lightly toasted bread)

1 tablespoon each of chopped parsley, ginger, coriander

1 teaspoon of chilli powder (mild or hot depending on taste)

50ml of milk

2 finely chopped garlic cloves

1 egg

Method:

Pre-heat the oven to 200 degrees (180C fan).

Fry the onions and garlic until they are golden. Turn off the heat and add the rest of the ingredients, stirring well.

Tip the mixture into a bowl and allow to cool slightly.

Roll into balls and place on a lined baking tray. ❄

Cook for 30 minutes, turning halfway through to allow to brown evenly.

These can be served on skewers or just picked from a warmed bowl using cocktail sticks.

Mods:

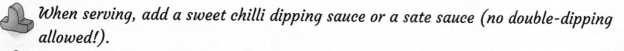

When serving, add a sweet chilli dipping sauce or a sate sauce (no double-dipping allowed!).

Add some Worcestershire sauce for extra flavour, or chilli flakes for heat.

The beef can be swapped for chicken or pork mince.

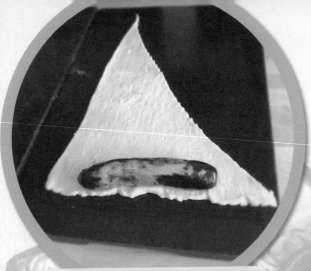

Getting Ready to Fold...

A "Natural 20"

When you roll and don't need modifiers for maximum success!

With bacon and cheese

Service!

Croissant Hot Dogs

Ingredients:

350g croissant dough (Jus-Rol dough makes 6, Pilsbury dough makes 8)

6/8 sausages

6/8 thin cheese slices (*optional)

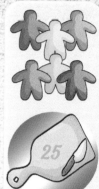

Method:

Pre-heat the oven to 200 degrees (180 for a fan oven) and line a tray with baking paper.

Brown the sausages (under the grill is slightly healthier than frying). Take the dough out of the fridge and separate out the pre-cut triangles.

Place the thin slice of cheese at the base of the triangle, place the sausage on top, then roll into a croissant shape.

Add an egg or milk glaze if required (see opposite for the difference a glaze makes). Place on the baking tray and cook for 12 to 15 minutes. Serve straight from the oven.

TIP: Keep the pastry in the fridge for as long as possible, if it gets too warm it will become unworkable

These can be eaten cold from the fridge the next day, but are best eaten as soon as they come out of the oven as they lose their flakiness as they cool.

Mods:

Thin herby sausages work best for this, and preferably ones that are not too long so you can still get a croissant shape to them.

They can be made with Frankfurter sausages, but you will need to boil the sausages first and drain them well before adding to the croissant dough.

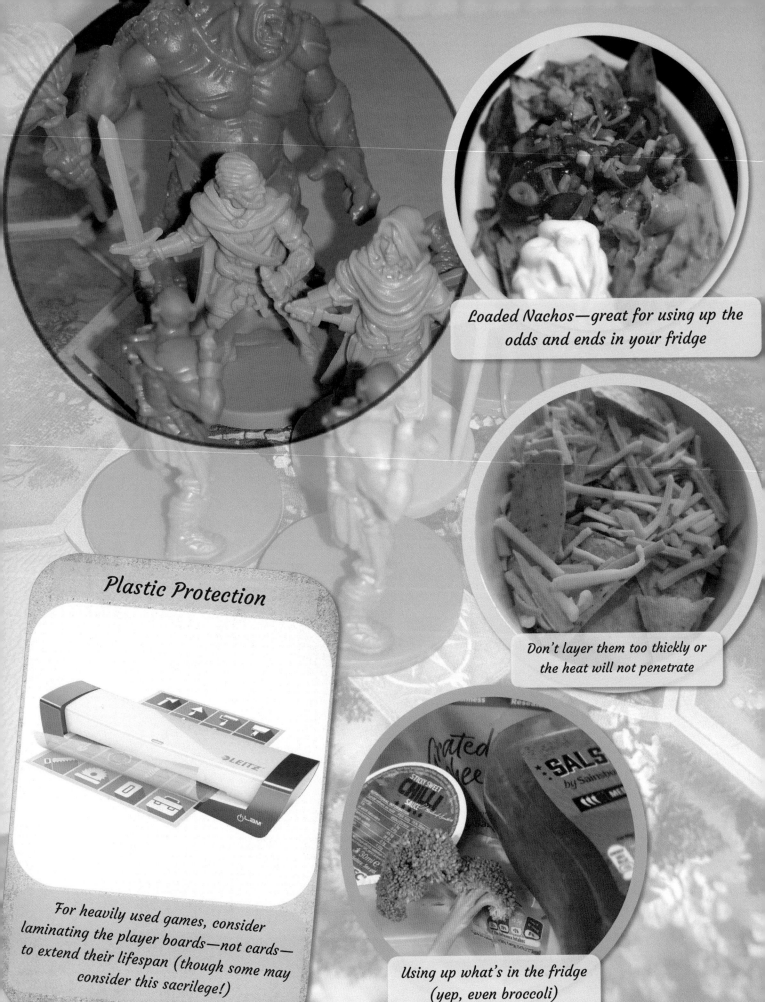

Loaded Nachos—great for using up the odds and ends in your fridge

Don't layer them too thickly or the heat will not penetrate

Plastic Protection

For heavily used games, consider laminating the player boards—not cards—to extend their lifespan (though some may consider this sacrilege!)

Using up what's in the fridge (yep, even broccoli)

Loaded Nachos

Ingredients:

175g plain tortilla chips

225g salsa

125g grated cheddar or Red Leicester cheese

4 spring onions, sliced

170g guacamole

150ml soured cream

3 Sliced red chillies, and jalapenos to taste

Method:

In each oven-proof serving dish, place the tortilla chips, salsa and spring onions. If you are confident in your guests tastes, you can add some sliced jalapenos and chillies at this point, otherwise serve them separately in side dishes so guests can add their own according to their tastes. Mix the ingredients gently a couple of times, then add the grated cheese over the top.

Place either in a hot oven (170 degrees) for 8 minutes, in a microwave for 60 seconds, or under a hot grill for 3 minutes. Serve immediately - remembering to warn your guests the dishes are hot!

These can be eaten cold from the fridge the next day, but are best eaten as soon as they come out of the oven as they lose their crispiness.

TIP: Do not prepare these too far in advance or you will end up with soggy nachos

Mods:

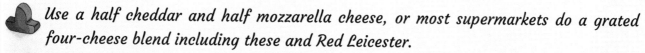 Use a half cheddar and half mozzarella cheese, or most supermarkets do a grated four-cheese blend including these and Red Leicester.

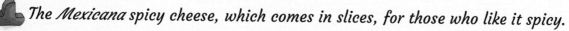 The *Mexicana* spicy cheese, which comes in slices, for those who like it spicy.

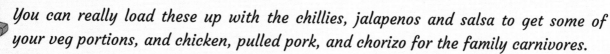 You can really load these up with the chillies, jalapenos and salsa to get some of your veg portions, and chicken, pulled pork, and chorizo for the family carnivores.

If you make them too large, they will deform, but are still perfectly edible

Edible Plates

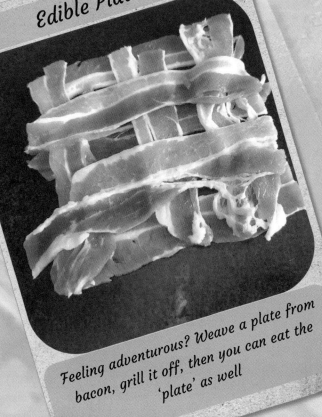

Feeling adventurous? Weave a plate from bacon, grill it off, then you can eat the 'plate' as well

Inclusivity

STRATA MINIATURES

D&D now has rules for combat wheelchairs—have a look at Strataminiatures.com for their awesome miniatures for adventurers

Crispy Mash Balls

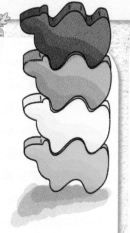

Ingredients:

4 cold mashed potatoes (see the potato skins recipe on page 23 if you want some mash)

100g grated cheese (cheddar or Red Leicester are great for this recipe)

1 large beaten egg

4 finely chopped spring onions

4 bacon rashers

100g bread crumbs

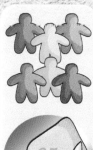

Method:

Fry the bacon and allow to cool, then cut into small pieces.

Mix the mash, egg, cheese, bacon, and spring onions in a bowl until combined.

Roll into small balls (around half an inch in diameter), coat in the breadcrumbs, then place in the fridge for 15 minutes.

Tip: If you want to freeze the mixture for later, freeze before adding the breadcrumbs.

In a frying pan, heat up 1/4 inch of oil until hot, then (very carefully) add the mash balls. Turn so they cook evenly, then remove using a slotted spoon, drain, and serve.

Mods:

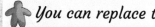 You can replace the bacon for ham hock or chorizo.

Add finely diced chillies for a bit of heat, or a sauce such as Worcestershire or Fire-cracker.

Planning on Proposing?

Incorporate your proposal (and ring) into a board game to pop the question

Freeze Your Cheese

Grate cheese and freeze it to make it last

They don't have to be round!!!

Mini-Cheese Carca-Scones

Ingredients:

100g grated cheese (a strong cheddar is ideal)

125g lightly salted butter

250g self-raising flour

Half a teaspoon of baking powder

150ml _full fat_ milk

Pinch of salt

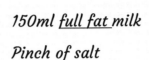

Method:

Pre-heat the oven to 200 degrees (180 for a fan oven).

Put the butter, flour, salt, and baking powder into a large bowl and gently rub together until it resembles breadcrumbs.

Slowly pour in the milk, mixing well as you do (take your time adding the milk).

Add the grated cheese and mix thoroughly to form your dough.

Roll the dough out on a flat surface until it is approximately half an inch thick, then cut-out circles.

Tip: With dough for scones, you do not want to overwork it. As soon as it forms 'breadcrumbs' slowly add the milk, then mix as little as possible to bring the dough together.

Brush the tops (only the tops, do not brush the sides as they will not rise properly) with milk, then bake in the oven until golden-brown (15 to 20 minutes). Serve with butter.

Mods:

Swap some of the cheddar cheese for Red Leicester to get a real glow to your scones.

To spice them up, add a pinch of cayenne pepper and a pinch of mustard powder.

Add spices rather than sauces so they do not become too moist.

You can use flatbreads as wraps...

Or cut them into strips to use as dippers

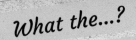

What the...?

Tile Laying: Where the map/playing area is built by players laying down terrain/building/location tiles

AP (Analysis Paralysis): 'If I play card A, then card E, then roll a dice... Or should I roll first?' When you overthink your turn/strategy so that you cannot decide what to do

Grognard: Someone who believes their first edition D&D is better than the latest edition (or any other game)

18xx: Games set in the 19th century, usually involving trains

MYO Butter

Herby, spicy, make-your-own (also called compound). Take plain unsalted butter, let it soften, then add your own ingredients: Garlic and truffle oil, English mustard, coriander and lime, even lemon. Portion it then chill or freeze it.

Flat-Bread of Winter

Ingredients:

250g plain flour

125ml warm water

2 tablespoons olive oil

A pinch of salt

Method:

Put the flour and salt into a bowl, then slowly add the water, mixing as you go until it forms a dough.

Add the olive oil and then knead until you have a soft, smooth dough (if it is too dry, keep adding drops of olive oil, if it is too wet add more flour).

Leave the dough to stand for 30 minutes.

Divide the dough into six balls, then roll them flat on a floured surface.

To a hot pan, add a tiny amount of oil (an oil spray is ideal for this), then cook each flatbread for 2 minutes on each side.

NB: Cooking these can produce a lot of smoke.

Mods:

If you prefer your flatbreads to be crispier, use a little more oil and cook them for 5 minutes on each side. Cook them in triangular shapes like this to make dippers.

Add a little rosemary or garlic to the dough at first mixing to give them a little more flavour.

Popcorn Maker

Cheap, easy-to-use, and child friendly, these are a great addition to a family kitchen for making healthy snacks.

Cheesy popcorn

Dice Cafe

Dice Board Game Lounge, Portsmouth.

A great place to try games and meet fellow gamers

Different varieties of popcorn are available

Savoury Popcorn

Ingredients:

Once you have popped your popcorn, here are some savoury serving suggestions:

Pepperoni Popcorn

For 200g of popped popcorn: take 10 slices of pepperoni and chop them finely. Gently fry the pepperoni until crispy (no oil required for the pan). Add a teaspoon of chilli powder, and black pepper to taste, and then the popcorn. Mix well in the pan and serve.

Peri Peri Popcorn

For 200g of popped popcorn: mix 1 teaspoon each of chilli flakes, paprika, garlic powder, dried rosemary, and oregano with a pinch of salt. Melt 50g of butter over a gentle heat, pour over the popcorn, then sprinkle on the spice mix, shake well, then serve.

Cheesy Popcorn

For 200g of popped popcorn: Combine 2 tablespoons of olive oil, 2 tablespoons of Italian seasoning and 1 tablespoon of garlic salt. Sprinkle this over the popcorn and shake well to coat the popcorn evenly. Add 100g of grated cheese and shake again.

Salt and Spice Popcorn

For 200g of popped popcorn: Combine 2 teaspoons of salt, 2 teaspoons of chili, half a teaspoon of cumin and half a teaspoon of ground black pepper. Sprinkle over the popcorn and shake well to coat evenly.

Pastry Meeples? Why not!

The story goes: The term 'Meeple' was first used by Alison Hansel during a game of Carcassonne in the year 2000. It is a portmanteau of 'my' and 'people'.

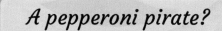

A pepperoni pirate?

Why not try adding features using cheese and pepperoni, or jam and lemon curd...

Sweet

Go easy on the chips!

Tempting as it is to add loads of chocolate chips to cakes, they will just sink to the bottom and break off in the tins.

Grate Your Butter

Don't have time to soften your butter? Grate it straight from the fridge and it be a lot easier to use, both in baking and on your toast.

Resources: Blue and honeycomb

Got an Idea?

There are plenty of different kits available if you are looking to design and make your own boardgame.

Toblerone Fudge

Resource Cube Fudge

Ingredients:

400g chocolate (broken up)

50g butter

297g Carnation condensed milk

125g icing sugar

Method:

Line a tin with baking paper—this recipe will fit perfectly in a 20cm square tin.

Put the chocolate, condensed milk, and butter into a non-stick pan and place on a low heat. Stir it every so often until it is thoroughly melted and mixed.

Sieve the icing-sugar into the mix whilst stirring well, then pour into the prepared tin and put it into the fridge. Leave for at least an hour until it has set and then cut into cubes.

This will last for up to two-weeks in the fridge, or up to a month in the freezer in a container.

Mods:

You can pretty much use any chocolate, though our particular favourites are Terry's Chocolate Orange and After Eights. If you have a really sweet tooth, go for white chocolate, though this can be very sweet. For a more balanced taste go for a darker chocolate.

You can also melt the mixture using a microwave, putting it in for 15 seconds and then stirring, repeating until the mixture is fully melted and smooth.

Adding ingredients into the fudge is simple enough, you do it after you have added the icing sugar. Raisins, mini-marshmallows, Rice Krispies, popping candy, sliced almonds, chopped cherries, and chocolate chips are just a few examples.

3 layers of joy!

Marbling with white chocolate

Bitesize

Buy pre-made chocolate cups and make your millionaire's shortbread in them!

You need to quickly freeze them between stages so the cups don't melt.

Quick Crumbs

If you need crumbs for a base, put the biscuits into a plastic bag, roll the top over, then beat them with a rolling pin, or the base of a pint glass, or a can of beans.

Millionaire's Shortbread

Ingredients:

250g sugar

275g plain flour

300ml condensed milk

50ml honey (runny, not set)

325g butter

1 large egg

200g dark chocolate

Method:

Preheat the oven to 180 degrees (160 fan).

Put the egg, 200g of the butter, and 100g of the sugar into a bowl and cream together until the mixture is fluffy.

Sieve in the flour and combine the mix until you have a dough.

Grease a rectangular baking tin and press the mixture firmly into the tin, forming an even base. Prick the base with a fork, and then bake for 10 minutes.

For the caramel, melt the remaining butter and sugar together and caramelise. Add in the condensed milk and honey, and allow to simmer for 20 minutes until the mixture is thick and well caramelised. Pour onto the base. Be careful not to burn it or it will taste bitter.

Allow the base to cool, then melt the dark chocolate (using a bain marie is the best option), and pour over the caramel. Leave to cool for an hour in the fridge.

Mods:

If you have children around you may find it easier to user a tin of ready-made caramel. Take a 397g tin of caramel and cook it in a pan on a medium heat for 7 minutes with 100g of butter and 100g of sugar.

257 Your torch lights up a large creature, seemingly made of rock itself, standing by the door

Don't overfill!

The icing sugar will be absorbed by the filling in the centre (see below)

Solo Play? You still need to eat!

Contentment +2

Raspberry, Lemon, and Lime

Lemon Puffs

Ingredients:

375g Puff Pastry

2 beaten egg yolks (optional)

200g Lemon Curd

Icing Sugar (to dust)

Method:

Pre-heat the oven to 200 degrees (180 degrees for a fan oven). Take a non-stick muffin/cake tray that will make 12 cakes.

Cut the pastry into 12 squares and then place a square into each mould in the tray. Add a dollop of lemon curd to the bottom of the cup. Brush the exposed pastry with the beaten egg-wash, then bake in the oven for 15 to 20 minutes until the pastry is golden brown.

Once cooled, remove from the tray, dust lightly with icing sugar, and place in a container in the fridge.

TIP: Do not eat these straight out of the oven, the sugar in the lemon curd will burn you!

Store in a container in the fridge for up to 3 days.

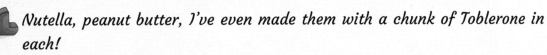

Mods:

You can use any curd or jam that has a thick consistency for this recipe, so check out your local farm shop to see what locally produced options they have.

Nutella, peanut butter, I've even made them with a chunk of Toblerone in each!

Quick Drip

When measuring out honey, syrup, or treacle, warm the spoon up first under the hot water tap. The syrup will then slide off the spoon more easily.

Some plain, some chocolate-dipped

Easy Baking Paper

Struggling to line a tin with baking paper? Cut a piece the right size, run it under the tap, then scrunch it up to dry it. It will now fold like cloth

Flapjacks

Ingredients:

300g jumbo porridge oats

125g brown sugar

125g unsalted butter

5 tablespoons golden syrup

Method:

Pre-heat the oven to 200 degrees (180 fan) and line a square tin (20cm) with baking paper.

Put the sugar, butter and golden syrup into a pan and melt over a low heat until the sugar has dissolved. Put the oats into a large bowl and pour the melted mixture over. Stir well until evenly combined.

Press the mixture into a baking tin, ensuring it is flat.

Score the top into the size portions you prefer, then bake in the oven for 15 minutes. Once cooked, leave to cool then cut into portions.

Mods:

The opportunities for modding flapjacks are huge:

- A common variation is to coat the top in melted chocolate. Do this after cooking and use a ratio of 4 parts chocolate to 1 part butter. Once the flapjacks are cooked and cooled, add the melted chocolate to the top and allow to cool again, then cut into pieces.

- You can swap 50g of the butter for peanut butter (crunchy or smooth).

- Try adding a pinch of ground cinnamon for the winter months.

- If you don't have golden syrup, you can replace it with runny honey or agave nectar.

Flapjacks are great for adding fruit to. Grated (and drained) carrot or apple, sultanas, dates, seeds such as pumpkin, and apricots.

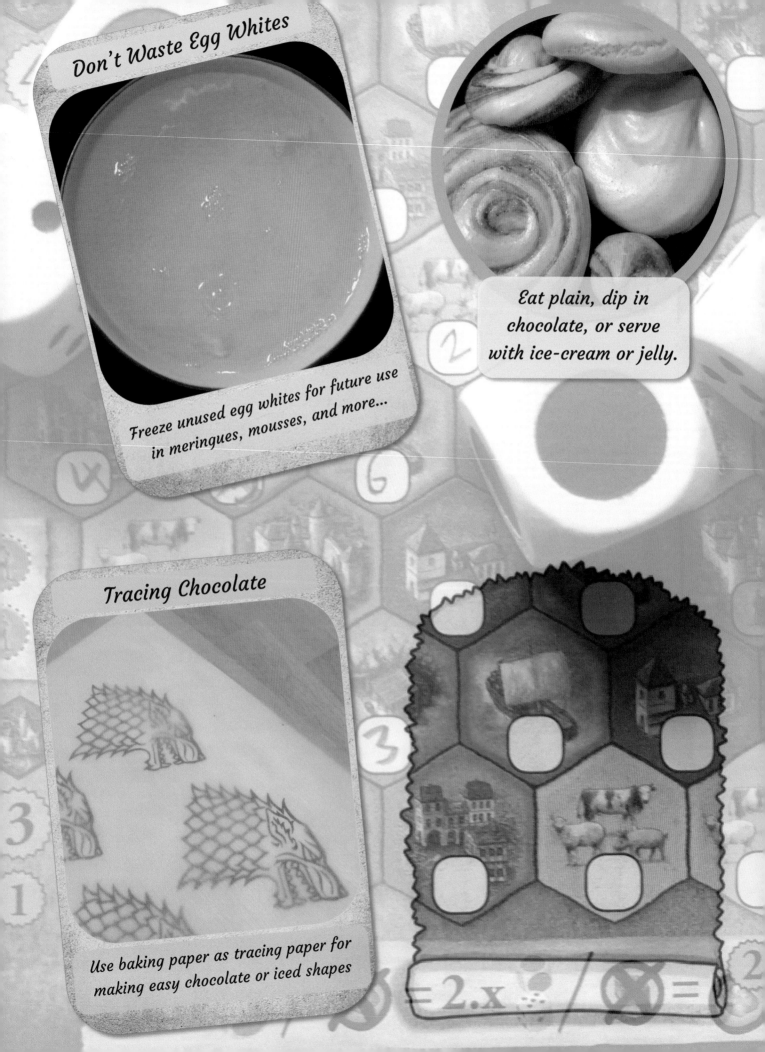

Don't Waste Egg Whites

Freeze unused egg whites for future use in meringues, mousses, and more...

Eat plain, dip in chocolate, or serve with ice-cream or jelly.

Tracing Chocolate

Use baking paper as tracing paper for making easy chocolate or iced shapes

Meringues

Ingredients:

4 large egg whites

115g sieved icing sugar

115g caster sugar

Food Colouring (Optional)

Method:

Pre-heat the oven to 100 degrees (yes, very low), and line a baking tray with non-stick baking paper.

Whip the egg whites until they form stiff peaks and then slowly add the caster sugar, a bit at a time. Once the sugar has been combined the mixture should be smooth and glossy.

Using a metal spoon, gently fold in the icing sugar a quarter at a time, and with the minimum amount of folding. When it is all combined, spoon onto the baking tray in artistic meringue swirls approximately three inches across (or blobs if you are like us) and bake in the oven for approximately one-and-a-quarter hours. They may need an extra 15 to 20 minutes in an older oven.

Mods:

You can add a swirl of red food colouring to make them more interesting to the eye, or drizzle them with melted chocolate once they have cooled.

If you want to make smaller, bite sized meringues they will only need approximately 50 minutes baking time.

Anything very finely grated, such as almonds or coconut, can be added to the mixture, as well as cocoa powder or flavour extracts (try not to add too much liquid as this will affect the integrity of the meringue, causing them to flop).

Cake Saver

When cutting cakes, push the end piece against the cut to keep the cake fresher for longer (this works for round cakes too)

Easy Decoration

Use a peeler or a grater for quick chocolate curls for muffins, tarts, and jellies

Cake Decorations

Break up chocolate bars for easy cake/muffin toppings

Grub...

Chocolate Muffins

Ingredients:

300g self-raising flour

80g sugar

2 eggs

1 teaspoon baking powder

50g butter

225ml milk

150g chocolate chips

1 teaspoon vanilla extract (optional)

Method:

Preheat the oven to 200 degrees (180 fan).

Put the flour and butter into a bowl and rub together until the mix resembles fine breadcrumbs.

Mix in the sugar and the cholate chips.

Tip: If you don't have chocolate chips, place a couple of your favourite chocolate bars into a bag and break them up with a rolling pin.

In a separate bowl, whisk together the eggs and milk (and vanilla extract if you are using it), then add to the dry ingredients and mix well.

Grease your muffin tin and pour evenly into each well (remember to leave enough space to a allow for the muffins to rise).

Bake for 18 to 20 minutes in the oven until cooked through (firm to the touch or you can use a knife to test).

Mods:

Add 50g of cocoa powder for double-chocolate, or swap the chocolate chips for blue-berries for something a little healthier. Decorate with walnut halves or pecans.

To give them a gooey centre, add a teaspoon of Nutella to the middle of the mixture just before you bake them.

Honey Biscuits

Micro Tip

Need a smaller amount of melted chocolate? Microwave in 15 second bursts, stir, and repeat until it melts.

Upgrade Time

Component upgrade kits, such as this one for Scythe, add life to your game.

With ground ginger and dipped in chocolate

Honey Biscuits

Ingredients:

75g unsalted butter

1 teaspoon bicarbonate of soda

75g sultanas or raisins (optional)

150g plain flour

350ml honey (runny, not set)

Method:

Pre-heat the oven to 180 degrees (160 fan) and line (or grease) a baking tray.

Put the flour and butter into a bowl and rub together until well mixed.

Using a tiny amount of hot water (a tablespoon is enough), dissolve the bicarbonate of soda and then stir into the flour and butter mix. If you wish to add sultanas or raisins then do so now.

Slowly pour the honey into the mixture stirring continuously as you do, until you have your finished biscuit dough. If it is too moist, slowly add more flour, if it is too dry, slowly add more honey.

Roll the dough out onto a floured surface until you have a sheet around about 1cm thick. Cut out the biscuit in your preferred shape and place them onto your baking tray. Cook for 12 minutes.

Mods:

Raisins or sultanas can be added, as mentioned, but also think about adding flaked almonds or a small amount of vanilla essence.

Try using different types of honey, such as forest for a less sweet taste, or orange blossom for a slightly fruity flavour.

Alternatively, add a tablespoon of ground ginger to the mix and dip in melted chocolate when cooked.

With swirls. Try sprinkling a chocolate flake on top...

A Bain Marie

You want a rough surface. The smoother it is the less swirl you will have

To melt chocolate, place a bowl over a pan a third full of water. Put it on a low heat and slowly melt your chocolate etc.

Overmixed it? Don't worry, it's 'just' a chocolate tart now!

Chocolate Swirl Tart

Ingredients:

200g digestive biscuits (or chocolate digestives)

200g plain chocolate

90g unsalted butter

250ml double cream

Method:

Crush the biscuits (the easiest way is to place them in a food bag and bash them with a rolling pin).

Melt the butter over a gentle heat and add to the crushed biscuits, making sure they are well mixed.

Tip the mixture into a 9" baking tin/pie dish and press down firmly until you have a compressed flat surface. Refrigerate for 30 minutes to allow the base to set.

Melt the chocolate (either in the microwave in 10 second bursts or by using a bain marie), then beat the cream until it is stiff.

Fold in the chocolate (3 or 4 folds, the more mixing the less 'swirl') and then pour over the base and chill for a further two hours.

Tip: A 'bain marie' to melt chocolate is where you third-fill a pan with water, rest a bowl over the rim (it must not touch the water) and put it on a low heat. You can then gently melt the chocolate (and other ingredients if the recipe requires) in the top bowl.

Mods:

Using different biscuits for the base - for example hobnobs - or a mix of biscuits such as swapping a few of them for amaretti biscuits, adds another layer of flavour.

This is also a recipe that is good for using up left-over Easter and Christmas chocolate. Instead of plain chocolate, try using a Terry's Chocolate Orange.

Need a Map?

Have a look at Inkarnate.com if you need mapping software to produce something for your campaign. Both free and paid options are available.

Nutella Popcorn

Cake Tins

Look for Bundt tins and madeleine tins to make more interesting cakes

Cinnamon Popcorn

Sweet Popcorn

Ingredients:

Once you have popped your popcorn, here are some sweet serving suggestions:

Chocolate Popcorn Squares

Grease a 20cm baking tray. Melt 200g of chocolate over a gentle heat. Add 150g of sweetened condensed milk, 50g of brown sugar, 100ml of water, and a pinch of salt. Turn the heat up and stir well until the sugar has completely dissolved. Take off the heat, add 200g of popcorn (already popped) and stir well, then pour the mixture into the baking tray and press down. Place in the fridge to cool for at least an hour, then cut into squares and serve.

Sugared Cinnamon Popcorn

For 200g of popped popcorn: melt 75g of butter, then add 100g of caster sugar, 2 teaspoons of ground cinnamon, and half a teaspoon of salt. Once everything has dissolved, pour over the popcorn and shake well to coat evenly.

Nutella® Popcorn

For 200g of popped popcorn: In a pan, combine 3 tablespoons of Nutella®, 50g of brown sugar, and a pinch of salt then warm over a gentle heat until the sugar has dissolved. Pour over the popcorn, shake well and serve.

Easy Caramel Popcorn

For 200g of popped popcorn: Gently warm 200g of Carnation Caramel (not the condensed milk, this is the easy version!) for 15 minutes. Add a pinch of sea-salt crystals (normal salt will do) and stir, then pour over the popcorn, shaking well to coat evenly, and serve.

Cut into squares...

Paste and fold...
(it doesn't have to be neat)

Gloomy Dungeon?

Go for some custom dice sets: glow in the dark? Galaxy Swirls? Heavy Metal? Cleric or Mage?

Cook and serve!

Chocolate Filo Straws

Ingredients:

25g butter

200g Nutella (or other chocolate spread)

220g Filo Pastry

Icing Sugar for dusting

Method:

Preheat the oven to 200 degrees (180 for a fan oven).

Melt the butter in a small saucepan then set to one side.

Cut a sheet of filo (a single layer, not multiple layers) into four rectangles and brush each with the melted butter.

Spread a tablespoon of chocolate spread down a short length, leaving a border to the side and the top and bottom.

Fold the top and bottom over, and the short side, then roll the straw up. Repeat to make 24 straws.

Place them on a baking sheet and bake for 12 minutes, then allow to cool. Gently dust with icing sugar and then serve.

Mods:

 Try using smooth peanut butter instead of Nutella

 For a nut free version, try filling with feta cheese and finely chopped mint, raspberry jam, or chorizo and cream cheese.

Shopping Look-outs...

Themed Moulds

For chocolates, icing, ice-cubes and more...

Themed Cutters

For biscuits, icing decorations, and pastry...

Token Organiser

Tidiness +3

A Perfect Fit

Have painted/assembled miniatures that need protecting in transport/storage? Look for laser cut ply and foam solutions.

Alcohol

All of the following recipes can be made with or without alcohol:

Present Idea

Food Pawn by Honeybadger Games

Tubes of Edible Meeples and Healing Potions

Cheat Card

Quarter lemons and limes, freeze them on a tray (or a plastic lid), then place them in a freezer bag. You now have ready made healthy ice cubes.

Adults only!

Dice-Cubes

Fruit juice (or vodka) rather than water as an alternative

Slanting Jellies

Making two-flavour shots? Let the first half set by putting them in a tray tilted on one side to add visual appeal

Vodka Jellies

Ingredients:

300ml vodka (chilled)

135g flavoured jelly cubes

475ml boiling water

175ml cold water

Method:

Break the jelly cubes into pieces and put into a large bowl. Add the boiling water, and stir until fully dissolved. Add the cold water and vodka and mix well.

Pour the mixture into shot glasses or ice-cube moulds, then freeze for at least 60 minutes.

Mods:

 There are plenty of jelly flavours available, such as orange, raspberry, strawberry, and blackcurrant, so you can create your own favourite flavours.

Alternatively, you can use flavoured vodka to create a mix of flavours, such as vanilla (goes well with raspberry jelly), or rhubarb (goes well with strawberry jelly).

The vodka can be substituted for gin, prosecco, tequila or rum (it will need longer to set with darker spirits).

Also, you can add fruits such as cranberries or strawberry slices.

You can also get vegetarian gel sachets to create a vegetarian option if required.

Smart Atmosphere

Have smartlights and Alexa/Google? Pre-program lighting effects such as "Alexa, open the dungeon", or "Google, the demon approaches".

Juice +2

Roll citrus fruits before juicing to get as much liquid as possible from them

Snacks Away

SULTANA
Galleon of the Chief Eunuch

...r to a Frontier. It gains Zeal ✠ +1.

The Chief Eunuch's Galleon was captured by Romegas whilst carrying the governor of Cairo and the nurse of Suleiman's daughter, Mihd... Proudly displayed in the harbour at M... a defiant trophy of war that flew i... Ottoman Empire

Limoncello Popcorn

Ingredients:

400g of popped popcorn

4 tablespoons of limoncello

Rind of 1 lemon

50g of butter

Juice of 1 lemon

Method:

Over a gentle heat, melt the butter, then add the limoncello and the lemon juice. Stir well, remove from the heat and add the lemon rind.

Pour onto the popcorn and shake well to coat it evenly. Allow to cool and then serve.

This can be stored in the fridge in an airtight container for up to three days.

Companies such as Cello (above) do a range of different 'cello flavours

Mods:

 'Cello's come in many flavours, not just lemon, so browse the supermarket shelves for a different flavour and pair it with the matching fruit for the juice and rind.

As well as lemon, look for orange, lime, strawberry, banana, and even chocolate.

Speak to Roll

Do you have Alexa or Google voice devices? "Alexa roll D20" or 'Google roll D6" will save you from getting RSI on your rolling wrist.

Early Starter?

The Thing - The Boardgame
Successful

Playmats and Bags for Board Games
Successful

Looking for new games before they come out? Have a look at Kickstarter, who have a variety of gaming related projects.

Dipping Time!

Tequila Guacamole

Ingredients:

3 finely chopped tomatoes

2 tablespoons of lime juice

3 avocados (peeled and de-stoned, 1 loosely chopped, 2 mashed)

1 chilli, finely chopped (better if de-seeded as well)

1/2 teaspoon of salt, cumin, cayenne pepper, and garlic powder

1 finely chopped red onion

2 tablespoons of tequila

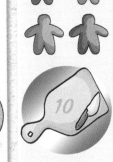

Method:

Mix everything together in a large bowl, then store in the fridge.

TIP: you could use shop-bought guacamole and just add the tequila

Use within 3 days of making.

Mods:

 You can try different/more chillies if you prefer it spicier.

 Try adding finely sliced kale, cherry tomatoes, or olives.

 For something slightly fruitier, sliced strawberries or pomegranate seeds.

D&D Beer

MODIST BREWING CO.
MINNEAPOLIS · MINNESOTA

Tabletop Session

ROLE PLAYING ADVENTURE
IN
NEW ENGLAND IPA

SEARCH FOR THE ELDER DRAFT AT
TABLETOPSESSION.COM

Independent brewers are becoming more creative with their packaging, so you may find a brew that meets your theme

Brownie Time

Leftover Wine?

Turn any leftover wine into ice cubes—not for drinking but for cooking, such as bourguignon or sausage casseroles

Whisky Brownies

Ingredients:

150g butter (unsalted)

150g light brown sugar

125g dark chocolate

125g self-raising flour

2 tablespoons whisky

2 eggs

125g caster sugar

120g icing sugar

Method:

Pre-heat the oven to 180 degrees (160 for a fan oven) and line a tray with baking paper.

Gently melt the butter and dark chocolate together, then mix in the brown and caster sugar until smooth. Add the eggs, one at a time, stirring well. Fold in the flour, taking care not to overwork the mixture.

Pour into the tin and bake for 30 minutes.

Once the tin has cooled, mix the icing sugar and whisky together and drizzle over the brownies. Cut into squares and serve.

Mods:

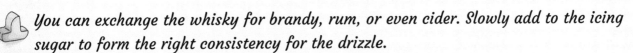You can exchange the whisky for brandy, rum, or even cider. Slowly add to the icing sugar to form the right consistency for the drizzle.

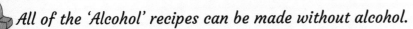All of the 'Alcohol' recipes can be made without alcohol.

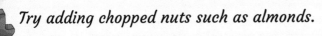Try adding chopped nuts such as almonds.

Dress for the Occasion

Look the part for your night with a theme: Carcassonne meeples? Catan hexes? D20 power plays?

Present Idea

CATAN

Themed phone, tablet, and laptop cases for the gamer in your life...

(Or to treat yourself)

Snacks Away

Accessibility

Several companies, such as 64ozgaames.com, do accessibility kits to replace all the flat components with accessible friendly versions

Rum Balls

Ingredients:

250ml whipping cream

100g milk chocolate, finely chopped

200g dark chocolate, finely chopped

25g unsalted butter, diced

2-3 tbsp dark rum

5 tbsp cocoa powder

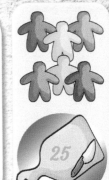

Method:

Warm the cream in a pan until just before it starts to boil. Pour the cream over the chocolate and keep stirring until the chocolate has fully melted and the mixture is smooth. Add the butter and the rum and mix in well.

Leave the mixture to cool, then cover and place in the fridge overnight (or for a minimum of four hours) so that the mixture sets.

Using a teaspoon, scrape out enough mixture to make a small ball, repeat until all the mixture is used, and then chill until you are ready to serve.

Sieve the cocoa powder into a shallow bowl, roll each ball (doing this as quickly as possible so it doesn't start to melt), in the cocoa powder to coat the outer surface.

Repeat until all the balls are covered and then serve.

Mods:

Roll them in melted chocolate instead of cocoa powder to give them a crispy shell.

Add finely ground coconut, or crushed walnuts.

Add some loosely broken chocolate biscuits when you add the rum and the butter to add some crunch.

These can be frozen for up to two months, or stored in the fridge for up to two weeks.

Not looking great...

But add the top layer...

Result

Stuck in a Lockdown?

Many games have online versions, either as apps for your phone or in Steam (Carcassonne above). Pandemic on the Xbox, anyone?

Baileys Chocolate Tiffin

Ingredients:

250g dark chocolate

250g milk chocolate

200g white chocolate

100g butter

300g shortbread (broken up)

5 tablespoons of Baileys Irish Cream

100g raisins

Method:

Leave the raisins to soak in the Baileys for at least 30 minutes. Line a baking tin with baking paper.

Combine 150g of each of the chocolates and the butter, and melt them.

In a large bowl, combine the dry ingredients and the raisins and Baileys. Add the melted chocolate to the bowl, stir well, then pour into the baking tin, pat down, and refrigerate for 30 minutes.

Melt the remaining 100g of each chocolate in separate bowls, pour in spots onto the top of the tiffin, then gently mix with a spoon to get the desired swirl effect.

Tap the tray several times to ensure the mixture settles flat, then chill.

Mods:

Try adding 200g of drained and quartered maraschino cherries, or go the sweeter route and add 200g of marshmallows.

Any chocolate bars can be broken up and added, and ones with a caramel filling work well (mars, snickers etc).

Ingredients:

Method:

Mods:

Ingredients:

Method:

Mods:

Ingredients:

Method:

Mods:

Ingredients:

Method:

Mods:

Notes

Quiz Answers Part 1

The following games provided the backdrops as we played and ate:

Page 6 Museum (2-4 players) by Holy Grail Games

Page 8 tiny epic dinosaurs (1-4 players) by Gamelyn Games

Page 10 Star Wars Outer Rim (1-4 players) by Fantasy Flight Games

Page 12 Unlock! Star Wars (1-6 players) by Space Cowboys

Page 14 Altar Quest (1-4 players) by Blacklist Games

Page 18 Dwarven Beerfest (2-4 players) by Triple Ace Games

Page 22 The Refuge: Terror from the Deep (1-6 players) by B&B Games Studio

Page 24 Zombie Dice (2-99 players) by Steve Jackson Games

Page 26 Castle Panic (1-6 players) by Fireside Games

Page 28 Dungeon Brawler (1-4 players) by Hypercube Games

Page 30 1750: Britain vs France (2 players) by Battle Hardened Games

Page 32 Gloomhaven Jaws of the Lion (1-4 players) by Cephalofair Games

Page 34 Star Trek Panic (1-6 players) by USAopoly

Page 36 Wakening Lair (2-6 players) by Rather Dashing Games

Page 38 Forbidden Island (2-4 players) by Gamewright

Page 40 Sushi Go! (2-5 players) by Gamewright

Page 42 Forest of Fate (2-6 players) by Cards of Fate

Page 44 Splendour (2-4 players) by Space Cowboys

Page 46 Sheriff of Nottingham (3-5 players) by Arcane Wonders

Page 48 Pet Evil (2-6 players) by PetEvil LTD

Page 50 Potion Explosion (2-4 players) by Horrible Games

Page 52 Runes of Mayhem (2 players) by Marzo Projects

Quiz Answers Part II

The following games provided the backdrops as we played and ate:

Page 54 LOTR Journeys in Middle Earth (1-5 players) by Fantasy Flight Games

Page 56 Memoir '44 (2-many players) by Days of Wonder

Page 58 Carcasonne (2-5 players) by Z-Man Games

Page 60 Dead of Winter (2-5 players) by Plaid Hat Games

Page 62 Celestia (1-6 players) by Blam!

Page 66 Terraforming Mars (1-5 players) by Stronghold Games

Page 68 Cleopatra and the Society of Architects (2-4 players) by Mojito Studios

Page 70 Fighting Fantasy Citadel of Chaos (1 player) by Steve Jackson

Page 72 Camel Up (2-8 players) by Pegasus Spiele

Page 74 Castles of Ravensburg (2-4 players) by Alea

Page 76 Black Seas (1-many players) by Warlord Games

Page 78 Black Fleet (2-4 players) by Space Cowboys

Page 80 Kingdom Builder (2-4 players) by Queen Games

Page 82 Pandemic Reign of Cthulhu (2-4 players) by Z-Man Games

Page 84 Forbidden Sky (2-5 players) by Gamewright

Page 88 UBOOT (1-4 players) by Phalanx

Page 90 1565 St. Elmo's Pay (1-2 players) by Tristan Hall

Page 92 Clear the Decks! (1-4 players) by Crispy Games Co.

Page 94 Mansions of Madness 2nd Edition (1-5 players) by Fantasy Flight Games

Page 96 D&D: Tomb of Annihilation (1-5 players) by Wizkids

Page 98 Atlantic Wolves (1 player) by Canvas Temple Publishing

Page 110 Codename Duet (2+ players) by Czech Games Edition

Keeping Score...

Round 1

Round 2

Round 3

Round 4

And the winner is:

108

Timing Notes

Week Before

Select Games

Send Invites (including directions and tutorials)

Check Crockery and Cutlery

Check Serving Dishes

Check Seating

Day Before

Marinade Meat/Tofu

Make Chilled/Frozen Desserts

Make Ice-Cubes

Check Game Components

Pre-Program Lighting

On The Day

-3:00 _____

-2:45 _____

-2:30 _____

-2:15 _____

-2:00 _____

-1:45 _____

-1:30 _____

-1:15 _____

-1:00 _____

-0:45 _____

-0:30 _____

-0:15 _____

Service!

Most Gifted...

Castle Panic. I must have gifted this at least seven times to friends with kids. It is a great co-op game to get the kids going, and can be played solo.

Current Favourite...

At the time of going to print, my current favourite is Mansions of Madness.

Always to Hand...

Zombie Dice. Perfect for small spaces: train tables, at the restaurant, on the bar. Quick, easy to play, and swap the tube for a velvet bag to make it super compact.

Parkin!

Must Have...

The one game you should have in your family collection: Sheriff of Nottingham.

Bonus: Parkin (My Favourite)

Ingredients:

120g treacle

170g butter

200g medium oatmeal

1/2 tsp ground nutmeg

1/4 tsp fine salt

1 egg

80g golden syrup

200g wholemeal flour

3 tsps ground ginger

175g brown sugar

1 tsp bicarbonate of soda

45ml milk

Method:

Pre-heat the oven to 160 degrees (140 fan) and line (or grease) a square baking tin.

In a pan, gently warm the treacle, syrup and the butter until it is melted through.

Combine the dry ingredients in a bowl, then add the treacle, stirring well until combined.

Mix the egg and the milk together, then add to the mixture. Mix, then empty the mixture into the baking tin.

Smooth, then cook for 90 mins. Take out of the oven and allow to cool in the tin for 30 minutes.

Mods:

There are no mods for this one, I've included it as my family favourite powerplay. If you're not familiar with parkin, it is best described as a rich gingerbread, traditionally from the north of England. There are plenty of regional variations, some more like a biscuit and others, like this one, more like cake. I love them all.

Printed in Great Britain
by Amazon